PUTTING-OFF
LIFE DOMINATING SINS

Susan Heck

DEDICATION

To my friend
Fonda Mauser
who faithfully challenges me
and others to put off sin.

If we claim to be without sin, we deceive
ourselves and the truth is not in us. If we
confess our sins, he is faithful and just and
will forgive us or sins and purify us from
all unrighteousness (1 John 1:8).

CONTENTS

INTRODUCTION

You have probably heard of Jonathan Edwards, who was one of the great preachers of the 18th century. However, you may not know the story of his daughter. Jonathan Edwards evidently had a daughter with an uncontrollable temper. It is said that when a certain young man came to ask Mr. Edwards for her hand in marriage his response was "no." The upset young man pleaded with Mr. Edwards.

"But I love her, and she loves me."

"That makes no difference," the girl's father responded. "She is not worthy of you."

"She is a Christian, isn't she?" the young man asked.

"Yes, she is," said Mr. Edwards, "but the grace of God can live with some people with whom no one else could ever live."

His daughter apparently had a problem with her temper. Jonathan Edwards's response indicated he knew that the presence of selfish anger indicates the absence of genuine love.

This true story illustrates many of the counselees who come to us for counseling. As Edwards said, it is only the grace of God that can live with some of these Christians, and it is only the grace of God that can change them.

As a biblical counselor, I wrote this booklet to be a resource for other biblical counselors. My publisher believed the material to be valuable as a self-evaluation tool for anyone who desires to live a life that brings the greatest glory to God. Song of Solomon 2:15 refers to the "little foxes that spoil the vines, for our vines have tender grapes." If we are to bear fruit for God's Kingdom, we must not let the 'little foxes' of life-dominating sin spoil the tender fruit. The sins mentioned here may seem 'small' and unimportant, but all sin is the same before God, and the axiom about the 'bad apple' spoiling the whole barrel is so true. That rotting apple goes unnoticed for a long time, quietly spoiling the rest of the fruit.

Paul told us in 1 Corinthians 10:13, *"No temptation has overtaken you except such as is <u>common</u> to man,"* (emphasis mine). What are some of the most common sins that plague Christians today? What are the biblical methods by which we can put off these sins? This booklet will give biblical definitions to common sins, as well as biblical helps and practical tips to motivate you to put off sin.

In preparing this material, I chose the top seven sins based on the counseling forms my counselees filled out in the last year. Now keep in mind that if one of these sins does not apply to you, *Seven Powerful Motivations for Putting off Sin* and *Seven Practical Helps for Putting Off Sin,* will be applicable no matter what sin you are committing. It is my prayer that this booklet will be scripturally profitable individually, in a small group study, or in the counseling room.

SEVEN PREDOMINATE SINS CHRISTIANS COMMIT

1. Can you guess the number one reason Christians seek counseling? You probably guessed it: **Depression**. Now, you might be asking, "Is depression a sin? Why, David was depressed, Elijah was depressed, and even Jesus was depressed…surely it can't be a sin." Depression per se is not a sin, but the choices many Christians make while they are depressed are sinful. The word for depression according to the Hebrew term means to be bowed down, incline oneself, and sink under the weight of sorrow. The Greek means grieved all around; intensely sad. It is interesting to note that in almost every Old and New Testament passage dealing with depression the answer is always the same: Trust in God. You will not find anti-depressants, food, sleep or any other such choices as answers to depression. Consider 1 Samuel 30:6: *"Now David was greatly distressed, for the people spoke of stoning him, because the soul of all the people was grieved, every man for his sons and his daughters. But David strengthened himself in the LORD his God"* (emphasis mine). Consider Psalm 42:11 and 43:5: *"Why are you cast down, O my soul? And why are you disquieted within me? Hope in God; for I shall yet praise Him, the help of my countenance and my God"* (emphasis mine). The Psalmist here could not even go to worship, more than likely because of illness. He was distressed, he was depressed.

Consider the following in Psalm 55, where David wrote about being so depressed and used terms such as, "my heart is pained," "fearfulness and trembling have overtaken me," "I am overwhelmed; I wish I had wings like a dove and then I would fly away." (In this context, David was writing these words because his good friend Ahithophel betrayed him) What was his response? *"Cast*

1

your burden on the Lord and He shall sustain you; He shall never permit the righteous to be moved" (v.22).

In Psalm 143, David was writing as he endeavored to escape from King Saul who was pursuing him. He ended up hiding out in a cave, and wrote about his spirit being overwhelmed, being brought down low, and that no one cared for his soul. What was his solution? Prozac? Suicide? No! *"Give ear to my prayer, O God."* (v.1) *"Attend to me and hear me."* (v.2) *"As for me, I will call upon God, and the LORD shall save me."* (v.16).

The last example of depression we should consider is our Lord in Mark 14:32-39. Here Jesus was facing the darkest hour of His life; crucifixion, separation from the Father, and the sins of the world placed on Him to the point that Isaiah said it pleased the Father to bruise Him, (Isaiah 53:10). Mark records in verse 34 that Jesus was exceedingly sorrowful even unto death. What was our Lord's solution to this great distress? He prayed and prayed and prayed, the Greek tense indicates. Over and over again the Lord prayed the following: *"Abba, Father, all things are possible for you. Take this cup away from me; nevertheless, not what I will, but what you will."*

Notice the ending of His prayer, *"not what I will, but what you will."* He relinquished His will to the Father to the extent that John records for us in John 18:11 that when Peter tried to cut off the ear of the high priest, Jesus told Peter to put up his sword. And then He said something very interesting, *"Shall I not drink the cup which my Father has given me?"* He committed Himself to the Father's Sovereign will in the depth of His depression. Depression itself is not a sin, but a lack of trust in God and His provisions found in His Word is sinful. Peter says in II Peter 1:3 that He has given us everything we need for life and godliness. Do you and I believe that?

2. Another common sin Christians commit is **bitterness** or **unforgiveness.** Bitterness in the New Testament is described as a "gall of bitterness" (Acts 8:23 KJV). Peter perceived that Simon the sorcerer had a heart of great wickedness and was "in the gall of bitterness, and in the bond of iniquity." Indeed, when we allow bitterness to grow in our heart it poisons our relationship with God and we become deeper in bondage to it. One who has a "root of bitterness" mentioned in Hebrews 12:15, is a wicked person with a sin that leads to denial of the faith. Unforgivenesss is when we do not excuse or pardon another in spite of our own shortcomings or errors. An unforgiving spirit and a bitter heart are terrible and common sins.

What does the Scripture say about this sin? Colossians 3:13 states, *"...bearing with one another, and forgiving one another, if anyone has a complaint against another; even as Christ forgave you, so you also must do."* We are to forgive as Christ forgave us, which means even as, according to, just as, in proportion to, in the same degree as He forgave. And how did Christ forgive us? Was it a partial forgiveness? Did He say, "Well, I will forgive you for that sin, but I can *never* forgive you for that one. That one is unforgivable." No, He forgave us fully and completely. The Lord's Prayer states in Matthew 6:12, *"and forgive us our debts, as we forgive our debtors."* We must forgive others completely because our Lord has forgiven us completely. *"Then Peter came to Him and said, "Lord, how often shall my brother sin against me, and I forgive him? Up to seven times"? Jesus said to him, "I do not say to you, up to seven times, but up to seventy times seven."* (Matthew 18:21, 22). That's 490 times! It is doubtful that we have ever forgiven someone that many times for the same offense! And yet the Lord has forgiven us 490 times plus more for the same offense that we repeat over and over!

There are other biblical examples we can follow as well. Let's look at Joseph in Genesis 50:19, 20, when his brothers

3

sought his forgiveness for selling him into slavery. He said, *"Am I in the place of God? But as for you, you meant evil against me; but God meant it for good, in order to bring it about as it is this day, to save many people alive."* Verse 21 says that he comforted them and spoke kindly to them. Look at Stephen in Acts 7:60, while he was being stoned to death, *"Then he knelt down and cried out with a loud voice, 'Lord, do not charge them with this sin.' And when he had said this, he fell asleep."* An unforgiving Christian is a contradiction of terms because we are the forgiven ones. Here are three practical steps to help you with unforgiveness:

1. Confess it to the Lord, and ask Him to help you mend the relationship.

2. Go to the person, ask forgiveness, and seek reconciliation.

3. Give the person something you highly value. This is a practical approach as Jesus said where your treasure is, there will your heart be also (Matthew 6: 21). You cannot ignore an unforgiving heart, as bitterness and resentment will set in, and will rob you of your joy. And by the way, an attitude of avoidance is not forgiveness.

3. **Gossip, slander, flattery and criticism** are in the third predominant category of sins Christians commit. These all have to do with our speech. Gossip is saying something behind someone's back that you would never say to their face, while flattery is saying to someone's face what you would never say behind their back. Gossip is idle talk that is not always true about other people. Yes, it is still gossip if is true. Flattery is praising too much or beyond the truth; it is to praise insincerely. These are common sins among women, but men are just as guilty.

Sometimes gossip falls into the category of slander. Slander is defaming, an evil report, wounding ones reputation by evil speaking. "Did you know that Sally's father abused her?" "Did you hear that Bill had his tenth car accident?" A good question to ask yourself before saying anything about anyone is this: "Would I say this if the person were standing here?" Or, "Do I need to say this and does this person need to hear it?" If the answer to these questions is 'no,' then you probably shouldn't say it.

Another form of ungodly speech is criticism. Criticism is unfavorable remarks or judgments; it is finding fault. A good example of this is when Moses sent forth the spies to observe the land that God gave to the nation of Israel, and they brought back an unfavorable report causing the whole community to grumble (Numbers 13:32). Another example is when Miriam and Aaron criticized Moses for marrying an Ethiopian woman (Numbers 12:1). A critical person rarely says anything good about anyone or anything. Perhaps a good reminder for us all would be to remember what Jesus said in Matthew 12:36, *"But I say to you that for every idle word men may speak, they will give account of it in the Day of Judgment."* In I Timothy 1:13 Paul wrote that before his conversion he was a blasphemer, but no longer, as he obtained mercy. Slander, gossip and the like must be put to death. (A good book to aid in helping in this area is War of Words by Paul Tripp).

4. **Coveting, jealousy and envy** are next on our list of life-dominating sins. Covetousness is the desire to possess more than we have, particularly that which belongs to someone else. Envy desires another's position, home or looks. It is wishing you had those things. Jealousy and envy are feelings of resentment towards another person because of his possessions or good qualities. This is what

causes fights according to James 4:1-4. *"Where do wars and fights come from among you? Do they not come from your desires for pleasure that war in your members? You lust and do not have. You murder and covet and cannot obtain. You fight and war. Yet you do not have because you do not ask. You ask and do not receive, because you ask amiss, that you may spend it on your pleasures. Adulterers and adulteresses! Do you not know that friendship with the world is enmity with God? Whoever therefore wants to be a friend of the world makes himself an enemy of God."*

One of the 10 commandments God gave Moses was this: *"You shall not covet your neighbor's house; you shall not covet your neighbor's wife, nor his male servant, nor his female servant, nor his ox, nor his donkey, nor anything that is your neighbor's"* (Exodus 20:17). For example, when a man or woman has a sexual relationship with one to whom he or she is not married, that is coveting; wanting something that is really not theirs to have. But that is only the beginning...

5. The fifth most common sins people commit are **sexual sins such as fornication, adultery, homosexuality and viewing pornography.** The Greek word for fornication is porneia (por-ni'-ah), from which we get our English word pornography. However in the New Testament, the word is broadened to include any kind of illicit sex. This would include every kind of immoral sexual relation. As we think about sexual sins, we must admit we are faced with temptation in a way that no other generation has seen because of the availability of pornography on the internet, television and magazines. I know of numerous families that have been ruined due to this terrible sin, much of which started on the computer.

The statistics are staggering! Internet Porn has a 57 billion dollar revenue world wide. 12 billion is United

States revenue, more than the combined revenues of all professional football, baseball and basketball franchises, of the combined revenues of ABC, CBS and NBC. 40 million people in the United States are sexually involved with the Internet. Sex is the number one topic searched on the internet. 25% of all search engine requests are porn related. These statistics should motivate you to guard yourself and your family. (Covenant Eyes is a great way to protect your family-www.covenanteyes.com).

So what does the Bible say about this awful sin? First of all in Matthew 15:19, Jesus tells us where this terrible sin comes from, *"For out of the heart proceed evil thoughts, murders, adulteries, fornications, thefts, false witness, blasphemies."* Paul tells us in 1 Corinthians 5:1 that *"It is actually reported that there is sexual immorality among you, and such sexual immorality as is not even named among the Gentiles—that a man has his father's wife!"* Paul says this type of fornication is not even practiced among the pagans and should not be practiced among Christians. He goes on to say in verse 11 of the same chapter: *"But now I have written to you not to keep company with anyone named a brother, who is sexually immoral, or covetous, or an idolater, or a reviler, or a drunkard, or an extortioner— not even to eat with such a person."* This leaves counselors with an awesome responsibility to begin church discipline if our counselee does not repent (Matthew 18:15-20). We as believers are not to be fellowshipping with those involved in this immorality. In Ephesians 5:3 Paul says *"But fornication, and all uncleanness, or covetousness, let it not be once named among you, as becometh saints."* Paul also tells us in 1 Corinthians 6:13b, *"Now the body is not for sexual immorality but for the Lord, and the Lord for the body."* We see in verse 18 of the same chapter that we are to *"flee sexual immorality. Every sin that a man does is outside the body, but he who commits sexual immorality sins against his own body."* In I Thessalonians 4:3 Paul says this: *"For this is the will of God, your sanctification: that you should abstain from sexual immorality."* Sexual sins are some of the hardest to break.

6. Sixth on the list of the most common sins Christians commit are **anger and wrath.** Anger is that which describes someone who is quick tempered, or exhibits violent passion or a deep smoldering bitterness. One man describes anger like this: "growing, inner anger, like sap in a tree on a hot day which swells the trunk and branches until they are in danger of bursting." If we would be truthful, we have all had that inner feeling of anger inside, some of us more than others. I had a real problem with anger before my new life in Christ. If you don't believe me, just ask my husband!

Wrath is indignation, the more abiding and settled habit of mind, like a roaring furnace. It describes a fierce passion (as if breathing hard). The Greeks would liken it to a fire in straw, which would flare up briefly and then be gone. What is the difference between wrath and anger? Anger often lies below the surface and gives rise to eruptions of wrath. Wrath is a boiling anger which often results in sudden outbursts of outrage. These things are extremely hurtful and I have counseled many women who are haunted by things they have said in a moment of anger. Who ever said, "Sticks and stones may break my bones, but words can never hurt me," must never have been the recipient of anger and wrath. A recent study revealed that murder is now the number one cause of death among pregnant women. This usually is caused by the anger or wrath of a husband or a boyfriend. This obviously is a sin that is not limited to gender.

We are living in a society that seems to be exploding with angry men, women, and even children. We have only to listen to reports of incidents associated with road rage to see how easily wrath can erupt in actions of drivers who

8

believe their 'rights' are being violated by others. These actions are examples of selfishness and pride.

Paul says in Colossian 3:8 that we are to put off anger and wrath. Ephesians 4:31 states: *"Let all bitterness, wrath, anger, clamor, and evil speaking be put away from you, with all malice."* In Matthew 5:22, Jesus says, *"But I say to you that whoever is angry with his brother without a cause shall be in danger of the judgment. And whoever says to his brother, 'Raca!' shall be in danger of the council. But whoever says, 'You fool!' shall be in danger of hell fire."* Psalm 37:8 is also very clear about our relationship to anger: *"Cease from anger, and forsake wrath; do not fret— it only causes harm."*

7. The seventh category of dominating sins committed by Christians includes **Lying, deception and hypocrisy.** What is lying? It means to utter an untruth or attempt to deceive by falsehood. Lying is all manner of hypocrisy and deception. Lying is from the devil, as Jesus says in John 8:44. It does not have anything to do with God, as Titus 1:2 states that He is a God who cannot lie. The Bible says that we come out of the womb speaking lies. Consider Psalm 58:3: *"The wicked are estranged from the womb; they go astray as soon as they are born, speaking lies."*

I will probably never forget a particular spanking my father gave me for lying. One Sunday morning before church we were all sitting at the breakfast table, all seven children and Mom and Dad. My dad asked me why I had a bandage on my cheek. I told him my brother had sliced my face with a knife. When he found out I had lied, he whipped the tar out of me, and I am grateful he did. As we grow from children to adulthood we become more sophisticated in our lying. People often pretend to be something they're not. They will pretend to be spiritual in church when they aren't at home; and that is a lie, and what is worse, their children and spouse see right through that. Not only will Christians lie, but they are teaching their children to lie by their example. When selling a house, a car, or any other personal item, many will lie about it. When the phone rings, people will tell their children to say mommy or daddy isn't home, when they are sitting right there.

Many people embellish stories to make them look good, or make the story interesting. That is an untruth, a lie. Others tell someone they will do something for them, or be there at a certain time, and fail to show up or are habitually late. That falls right in the category of lying.

If a person will lie and be comfortable with lying, he or she will fall to any temptation, and they never have to fear being discovered because they are so good at deception. Paul says in Ephesians 4:25, *"Therefore, putting away lying, let each one of you speak truth with his neighbor for we are members of one another."*

Now, before we go on to the next section, you might be wondering why I did not list marriage problems as one of the seven predominant sins. It is indeed a major topic in counseling, and most of the seven sins I just mentioned can be a result of marriage difficulties. Marriage difficulties can cause many Christians to be depressed, to be angry, to get involved in sexual sin, to lie and be deceptive, to have deep rooted bitterness and unforgiveness towards their spouse, to be involved in ungodly speech and in some cases (especially if adultery has taken place) to be envious or jealous.

Let's take a look at the Seven Powerful Motivations for Putting Off Sin.

SEVEN POWERFUL MOTIVATIONS FOR PUTTING OFF SIN

Paul says in Colossians 3:5, *"Therefore put to death your members which are on the earth: fornication, uncleanness, passion, evil desire, and covetousness, which is idolatry."* Put to death means to subdue, to deaden, to kill, to reckon as dead. We are to make a corpse of sin, deprive it of power, and destroy the strength of it. The Greek tense indicates to do it now! Don't put it off. As Christians we do not have the luxury of being apathetic about sin in our lives. Some people say they are gradually weaning themselves from a certain sin, but that is absurd. Where is that in the Bible? Romans 6:1-15 tells us something a little different.

[1]What shall we say then? Shall we continue in sin that grace may abound? [2]Certainly not! How shall we who died to sin live any longer in it? [3]Or do you not know that as many of us as were baptized into Christ Jesus were baptized into His death? [4]Therefore we were buried with Him through baptism into death, that just as Christ was raised from the dead by the glory of the Father, even so we also should walk in newness of life. [5]For if we have been united together in the likeness of His death, certainly we also shall be in the likeness of His resurrection, [6]knowing this, that our old man was crucified with Him, that the body of sin might be done away with, that we should no longer be slaves of sin.[7] For he who has died has been freed from sin.

⁸Now if we died with Christ, we believe that we shall also live with Him, ⁹knowing that Christ, having been raised from the dead, dies no more. Death no longer has dominion over Him. ¹⁰For the death that He died, He died to sin once for all; but the life that He lives, He lives to God. ¹¹Likewise you also, reckon yourselves to be dead indeed to sin, but alive to God in Christ Jesus our Lord.

¹²Therefore do not let sin reign in your mortal body, that you should obey it in its lusts. ¹³And do not present your members as instruments of unrighteousness to sin, but present yourselves to God as being alive from the dead, and your members as instruments of righteousness to God.¹⁴For sin shall not have dominion over you, for you are not under law but under grace.¹⁵What then? Shall we sin because we are not under law but under grace? Certainly not!¹⁶Do you not know that to whom you present yourselves slaves to obey, you are that one's slaves whom you obey, whether of sin leading to death, or of obedience leading to righteousness?

Paul says we are to put to death our members. What does Paul mean by members? A limb or part of the body? It refers to whatever belongs to your earthly nature. One translation puts it this way "kill all your animal appetites." How are we going to be convinced to put off these sins? Well, let's look at Seven Powerful Biblical Motivations for putting sin to death!

1. **The wrath of God is coming on the disobedient**. Paul says in Colossian 3:5 and 6: *"Therefore put to death your members which are on the earth: fornication, uncleanness, passion, evil desire, and covetousness, which is idolatry. Because of these things the wrath of God is coming upon the sons of disobedience."* The words "is coming" are in the present tense and suggest that God's wrath has already begun and will culminate in the future. Wrath in the Greek in this context is a word for violent passionate punishment. (See John 3:36, Romans 1:18-2:11, Romans 2:5 Ephesians 5:3-6; and II Thessalonians 1:7-9.)

A good example of this would be what Paul says in Hebrews 13:4: *"Marriage is honorable among all, and the bed undefiled; but fornicators and adulterers God will judge."* This suggests that God's wrath will come at some time upon those who commit sexual sin.

In the Colossians passage above, Paul warns that this wrath, this anger of God has come and will come on the sons of disobedience. Disobedient is a word that describes the obstinate and rebellious. This would indicate that God sees us as sons of disobedience if we are involved in these sins. God is holy and cannot allow sin; therefore His wrath comes because of sin.

I think we can see even today some manifestation of the wrath of God that has come upon us as a nation, and it is no wonder when you consider what the average Christian believes. A survey among professing Christians revealed that 97% believe God is forgiving, 96% believe He is loving, but only 37% believe that God is judging, and only 19% believe He punishes those who do wrong. I am always amazed at people who tell me they have no fear of disobeying God. I can assume they do not take God seriously and have no fear of judgment. If we don't take God seriously, then how can we safely say we take our marriage seriously, the raising of our children seriously, faithfulness, sexual purity, humility, repentance, honesty, lying, cheating, stealing, and the like?

2. **These sins are an indication of the old life.** We are dead to self and alive with Christ. Again, Paul says in Colossians 3:3: *"For you died, and your life is hidden with Christ in God."* The word dead comes from the Greek word *apethanete* which refers to a definite act. "You died", Paul says. Your former life died, and all the evil of it, when you came to Christ. You are dead to your self and you are dead to sin. It is just like someone who is dead physically; they don't care what you do with their earthly possessions, they are dead! We need to consider ourselves dead to the things of this world, just as a dead corpse is dead to earthly entrappings.

> *...that you <u>put off</u> concerning your former conduct, the old man which grows corrupt according to the deceitful lusts, and be <u>renewed</u> in the spirit of your mind, and that you <u>put on</u> the new man which was created according to God, in true righteousness and holiness* (Ephesians 4:22-24, emphasis mine).

3. **Those who practice these things will not inherit the kingdom of heaven.** The following passages are very clear about this fact. Just so you don't miss the impact of these verses, read them out loud. Then ask yourself, "What does that say?" "What does that mean?" Some people are under the delusion that they can retain their sin and go to heaven.

> *<u>"Do you not know that the unrighteous will not inherit the kingdom of God?</u> Do not be deceived. Neither fornicators, nor idolaters, nor adulterers, nor homosexuals,*

14

nor sodomites, nor thieves, nor covetous, nor drunkards, nor revilers, nor extortioners will inherit the kingdom of God. And such were some of you. But you were washed, but you were sanctified, but you were justified in the name of the Lord Jesus and by the Spirit of our God" (1 Corinthians 6:9-11, emphasis mine),

"Now the works of the flesh are evident, which are: adultery, fornication, uncleanness, lewdness, idolatry, sorcery, hatred, contentions, jealousies, outbursts of wrath, selfish ambitions, dissensions, heresies, envy, murders, drunkenness, revelries, and the like; of which I tell you beforehand, just as I also told you in time past, that <u>those who practice such things will not inherit the kingdom of God"</u> (Galatians 5:19-21, emphasis mine).

"He who sins is of the devil, for the devil has sinned from the beginning. For this purpose the Son of God was manifested, that He might destroy the works of the devil. Whoever has been born of God does not sin, for His seed remains in him; and he cannot sin, because he has been born of God. In this the children of God and the children of the devil are manifest: <u>Whoever does not practice righteousness is not of God,</u> nor is he who does not love his brother" (1 John 3:8-10), emphasis mine).

15

"But the cowardly, unbelieving, abominable, murderers, sexually immoral, sorcerers, idolaters, and all liars <u>shall have their part in the lake which burns with fire and brimstone,</u> which is the second death" (Revelation 21:8, emphasis mine).

4. **The Lord's Return.** The Lord's return should be motivation for holy living. Read 1 John 3:1-3: *"Behold what manner of love the Father has bestowed on us, that we should bé called children of God! Therefore the world does not know us, because it did not know Him. Beloved, now we are children of God; and it has not yet been revealed what we shall be, but we know that when He is revealed, we shall be like Him, for we shall see Him as He is. And everyone who has this hope in Him purifies himself, just as He is pure."*

Also, Colossians 3:4: **"When Christ who is our life appears, then you also will appear with Him in glory."** And yet another passage: 1 Thessalonians 4:14-18, *"For if we believe that Jesus died and rose again, even so God will bring with Him those who sleep in Jesus. For this we say to you by the word of the Lord, that we who are alive and remain until the coming of the Lord will by no means precede those who are asleep. For the Lord Himself will descend from heaven with a shout, with the voice of an archangel, and with the trumpet of God. And the dead in Christ will rise first. Then we who are alive and remain shall be caught up together with them in the clouds to meet the Lord in the air. And thus we shall always be with the Lord. Therefore comfort one another with these words."*

Revelation 20:11-15 is another very sobering passage to be reminded of regarding our sin and the fact of the Lord's coming: *"Then I saw a great white throne and Him who sat on it, from whose face the earth and the heaven fled away. And there was found no place for them. And I saw the dead, small and great, standing before God, and books were opened. And another book was opened, which is the Book of Life. And the dead were judged according to their works, by the things which were written in the books. The sea gave up the dead who were in it, and Death and Hades delivered up the dead who were in them. And they were judged, each one according to his works. Then Death and Hades were cast into the lake of fire. This is the second death. And anyone not found written in the Book of Life was cast into the lake of fire."* The fact that the Lord is coming should motivate us to live a holy life.

5. **Ongoing sin has terrible consequences.** There are many examples in Scripture of sin and its awful consequences. Read and study Deuteronomy 28 looking for all the cursings of disobedience and blessings of obedience. Deuteronomy has a list of cursings for those who disobey and blessings on those who obey. It describes blessings such as good health, increasing crops and blessings on their children, while cursings include bad health and death, no crops and lack of peace in their lives.

Another sobering passage of sin's consequences is found in Acts 5:1-11 where we have the account of Ananias and Sapphira who were struck dead for lying to Peter and the apostles and the Holy Spirit. King David's child was taken when it was only seven days old because of David's sin with Bathsheba (2 Samuel 12). Paul mentions some who are sick and have even died in 1 Corinthians 11:27-32 because they have come to the Lord's Table with sin in their life and have brought judgment on themselves.

Others to consider are: The story of Cain and Abel in Genesis 4, King Ahab and Jezebel in 1 and 2 Kings, and the story of Jonah in the book of Jonah. We also have consequences of sin mentioned in Matthew 18:15-20 which deals with rebuking Christians in sin and those who do not repent are eventually put out of the church. These are very serious consequences to consider when putting off life-dominating sins.

6. **Sin grieves the Holy Spirit and is displeasing to God.** The sins we continually commit and refuse to put off cause us to quench God's Spirit in our life and hinder our growth. They are displeasing to God. It is just like a child who continually disobeys his parents without changing; it is grievous! Ephesians 4:30 tells us: *"And do not grieve the Holy Spirit of God, by whom you were sealed for the day of redemption."* 1 Thessalonians 5:19 commands: *"Do not quench the Spirit."* 1 John 2:3-4 says: *"Now by this we know that we know Him, if we keep His commandments. He who says, "I know Him," and does not keep His commandments, is a liar, and the truth is not in him"* (emphasis mine). And later on John will say in I John 3:22-24, *"And whatever we ask we receive from Him, because we keep His commandments and do those things that are pleasing in His sight. And this is His commandment: that we should believe on the name of His Son Jesus Christ and love one another, as He gave us commandment. Now he who keeps His commandments abides in Him, and He in him. And by this we know that He abides in us, by the Spirit whom He has given us."*

7. **Sin gives a foothold to Satan.** 1 Peter 5:8-9 gives us warning here regarding our enemy, the devil and says: *"Be sober, be vigilant; because your adversary the devil walks about like a roaring lion, seeking whom he may devour. Resist him, steadfast in the faith, knowing that the same sufferings are experienced by your brotherhood in the world."* Peter may have been recalling what his Lord said to him in Luke 22:31-32. *"And the Lord said, 'Simon,*

Simon! Indeed, Satan has asked for you, that he may sift you as wheat. But I have prayed for you, that your faith should not fail; and when you have returned to me, strengthen your brethren."'

Paul also mentions the danger of our enemy in his writings to the church at Ephesus. Ephesians 4:26-27 says *"Be angry, and do not sin: do not let the sun go down on your wrath, nor give place to the devil."* Ephesians 6:11-12, *"Put on the whole armor of God, that you may be able to stand against the wiles of the devil. For we do not wrestle against flesh and blood, but against principalities, against powers, against the rulers of the darkness of this age, against spiritual hosts of wickedness in the heavenly places."* Christians need to understand that we have an enemy who would like to devour us and render us useless to God. If we don't repent from sin, Satan will entrap us and leave us defeated.

Now that we have given Seven Biblical Motivations to put off sin, let's finish with some practical tips for putting off sin.

SEVEN PRACTICAL TIPS FOR PUTTING OFF LIFE-DOMINATING SIN

1. **Scripture Memorization**. Hebrew 4:12 reminds us, *"For the word of God is living and powerful, and sharper than any two-edged sword, piercing even to the division of soul and spirit, and of joints and marrow, and is a discerner of the thoughts and intents of the heart."* I can honestly say that this is the one area I have seen the Lord use over and over again to change Christian's lives. For a closer look at the importance of Scripture memorization you can obtain my booklet, "A Call to Scripture Memory" from www.focuspublishing.com

Scripture Memorization helps you to hide God's Word in your heart so you do not sin against Him. *"Thy word have I hidden in my heart, that I might not sin against thee"* (Psalm 119:11). Also Psalm 37:31 says hiding God's Word will keep your steps from sliding. *"The law of God is in his heart; none of his steps shall slide."* As you memorize God's Word you are forced to go over and over it again. Many verses that perhaps we gloss over in our everyday reading will suddenly jump out at us, and—ouch—we are faced with our sin.

Romans 12:1-2 says, *"I beseech you therefore, brethren, by the mercies of God, that you present your bodies a living sacrifice, holy, acceptable to God, which is your reasonable service. And do not be conformed to this world, but be transformed by the renewing of your mind, that you may prove what is that good and acceptable and perfect will of God."*

There is no better way to renew your mind than with the Word of God. Scripture memorization will transform your mind and you will begin to look at life differently, you will look at God and others differently, and you will handle situations differently.

2. **Journaling.** Begin by writing down the things that are causing you to be depressed, to be angry, etc. This could be circumstances or people. Then journal what you are thinking when you are feeling this way. You will usually discover it is unbiblical thinking. Next, journal what you should be thinking under these circumstances. Be sure to include the right thinking in your journal. The Self Confrontation Manuel (John Broger) has worksheets which I have found to be very helpful. Also, Transformed into His Likeness by Armand Tiffe charts 106 behaviors to Put Off and the corresponding behaviors to Put On with appropriate Scripture references. Colossians 3 is a great place to find help to know what we are to put off and what we are to put on. For example: Forbearance in place of fighting and unforgiveness; telling the truth in place of lying; longsuffering instead of outburst of anger or wrath.

3. **Fasting and Praying**. Ask yourself how much you have prayed about your problem. Have you ever fasted? I often ask women who come in for counseling, "How much have you prayed about this problem?" What is interesting is that most will respond with, 'not much' or 'not at all.' Philippians 4:6 says we are not to be anxious but to pray about everything. In Matthew 17:21, Jesus was speaking with the disciples as to why they could not cast a demon out of a man, *"This kind does not go out except by prayer and fasting."* My new book, With The Master on Our Knees, will have two chapters devoted to this often neglected topic of prayer and fasting. I am convinced we don't see more

victory in our lives because we do not pray and fast. Make sure you allow time each day for prayer, and be willing to fast about your situation.

4. **Call sin 'sin'.** Psychological terms have become very common in everyday conversation. Be aware of this and don't use psychologized terms such as 'addiction', 'bi-polar', 'self-esteem' and 'dysfunctional'. Instead of self-esteem, use the terms loving yourself or selfishness. Paul tells us in Philippians 2:4 that we are not even to think of our self at all, but to scope out the interests of others.

Instead of using the term bi-polar, use the word anger. Instead of dysfunctional use the term, 'sinful'. Instead of saying, "I had an affair," you must speak the truth, "I committed adultery." You might want to say, "I told a white lie," but you should say, "I lied." Instead of saying, "I was a little frustrated with my spouse," what you mean was, "I was angry!" Do not minimize your sin. When you do, you don't see the seriousness of your sin and you have no hope. Practice this form of telling yourself the truth by recording it in your journal. With God there is hope, with psychologized terms there is no hope.

5. **Find someone to hold you accountable for your sins.** James 5:16 says, *"Confess your sins to one another and pray for one another, that ye may be healed."* Find another Christian you trust and respect (of the same sex) to be your accountability partner. Perhaps he or she will want to go through this process with you. You can designate written or oral assignments to be turned in to your partner. Some suggestions are Scripture passage reading, Scripture memorization, Christian living books to read and discuss, practical practice of the Put-off/Put-On principle: put off (a specific sin) and put on (Scripture-related godly character). If you are not willing to put some effort into doing practical assignments, you probably are not serious about change.

6. **Go the Extra Mile.** We all live busy lives and at times it seems there aren't enough hours in the day to get everything done. However, I would challenge you to join a weekly Bible study or Sunday school class, or become involved in a mentoring relationship. Be sure with each of these that Scripture is the final word so that you will not be at risk of being "tossed here and there by waves, and carried about by every wind of doctrine" (Ephesians 4:14). If we don't study the Word and the teachings of our Lord, we fall into a pattern of setting our own standard of holiness. God's standard is high and holy and He is faithful to give us discernment through His Word. Determine to be obedient to God's Word.

If you do join a Bible study or become involved in a Sunday school class, try to find a group that is fairly small and where members are willing to hold one another accountable. A word of caution: It is easy for a small group of people to get distracted by idle chatter, so you must be one who will contribute to keeping things on task.

7. **Make sure you are truly redeemed.** If after a reasonable amount of time, you are not obtaining victory over sin, go over the issues of salvation with your Christian accountability partner, pastor or biblical counselor. Do you truly have a heart for God, His Word, and spending time in prayer? Do you have a heart of repentance over your sin? Issues of the gospel, repentance, and the Lordship of Christ in your life should be thoroughly thought out and discussed.

Following the conclusion are some tests of faith from James and I John that will aid in discovering where one's heart genuinely is.

Conclusion

It is my deepest desire to help Christians put off life dominating sins and put on life changes that are Christ like. If you were the daughter of Jonathan Edwards, I trust that with these biblical helps Mr. Edwards would not need to say to a prospective husband, "No, you cannot have her; you see she has a temper, and worse than that, she is given over to outbursts of anger. No, you cannot have her, she is bent on evil and involved in gossip and blasphemy and every once in awhile she comes up with the dirtiest jokes that aren't even fit for a sailor to tell. No, you can't have her; she cannot be trusted to tell the truth."

I trust that instead you would hear from the lips of not only your earthly father, but more importantly, from your Heavenly Father, "Yes, you can have her; she will do you good and not evil all the days of her life. She is full of compassion, kindness, and gentleness. She can be fully trusted—she is an honest woman. She is a virtuous woman, and her price is far above rubies. She will make you a good bride, as her actions show she is a part of the Bride of Christ."

And what would Mrs. Edwards say of her son? "He is a genuine man of God. He is a man of integrity and honesty; one who strives to emulate his Savior and Lord Jesus Christ.

TESTS OF FAITH - FROM JAMES

Tests of Faith – James 1

1. Do you count your trials with joy? (v 2)
2. Do you see your trials as something that God uses to perfect your faith and develop patience? (v 4)
3. Do you ask God for wisdom in trials, and do you ask in faith? (v 5)
4. If you don't have too much money today, are you still joyful in your God? (v 9)
5. If you have an abundance of money today, do you recognize your wealth as a gift from God, and do you see your life as fleeting regardless of your wealth? (vv 10-11)
6. Do you endure trials? (v 12)
7. Do you blame God for your temptations? (vv 13-14)
8. Do you recognize the many gifts that God has poured out on you and are you grateful? (v 17)
9. Are you swift to hear, slow to speak and slow to get angry at the Word of God, or to those who proclaim it? (v 19)
10. Have you put away all filthiness and wickedness from your life? (v 21)
11. Do you receive the Word with meekness? (v 21)
12. Are you a doer of the Word, or just merely a hearer (an auditor)? (v 22-25)
13. Do you continue in the Word, or are you haphazard in your time with God? (v 25)
14. Do you keep a tight reign on your tongue? (v 26)
15. Do you minister to the orphans and widows? (v 27)
16. Are you keeping yourself unspotted from the world? (v 27)

Tests of Faith – James 2

1. Do you show favoritism to any class of people—poor or rich? (v 1-10)
2. Do you love your neighbor as yourself? (v 8)
3. Is your life characterized by showing mercy? (v 13)
4. Does your faith show itself by your works? (v 14-26)
5. Do you help the destitute brother or sister? (v 14-17)

Tests of Faith – James 3

1. If you have the gift of teaching, have you rushed into that office? (v 1)
2. If you have the gift of teaching, do you study hard to interpret Scripture accurately, and does your life measure up to what you teach? (v 1)
3. Do you bless God and curse others with the same mouth? (v 10)
4. Does your life manifest a life of wisdom? (v 13-18)
5. Do you prove yourself to be wise by an upright life? (v 13)
6. Do you have bitterness, envy, or strife in your heart? (v 14-16)
7. When you speak and give advice, is it pure, peaceable, gentle, willing to yield, full of mercy and good fruits, without partiality and without hypocrisy—or is it earthly, sensual, and demonic? (v 14-18)
8. Are your fruits of righteousness sown in peace? (v 18)

Tests of Faith – James 4

1. Are you known as a person who argues? Do you always have to have things your way? (v 1-3)
2. Do you pray for selfish desires? (v 1-3)

3. Are you a friend of the world? (v 4)
4. Is your life characterized by humility? (v 6)
5. Do you submit to God? (v 7)
6. Do you resist the devil? (v 7)
7. Do you draw near to God? (v 8)
8. Do you weep and mourn over your sins? (v 9)
9. Do you speak evil of others and judge others? (v 11)
10. Do you make plans without consulting the Lord? (vv 13-16)
11. Are you a proud and boastful person? (v 16)
12. When you know that something is right, do you do it? (v 17)

Tests of Faith – James 5

1. Do you live for pleasures on this earth? (v 5)
2. Are you oppressive towards those who are less fortunate than you? (vv 4, 6)
3. Are you patient towards those who afflict you? (v 6)
4. During afflictions, do you establish (prop up) your heart? (v 8)
5. Do you murmur against others during afflictions? (v 9)
6. Does your yes mean yes, and your no mean no? Can your word be trusted? (v 12)
7. Do you make rash vows? (v 12)
8. Do you pray in affliction? (v 13)
9. Do you sing when you're merry? (v 13)
10. When you're sick, do you call the spiritual leadership to come and pray for you? (v 14)
11. When you are sick, do you search your heart for sin? (v 15)

12. Do you confess your sins to those you have wronged? (v 16)

13. Do you have someone that you are accountable to; someone to pray with and with whom you can share your real struggles? (v 16)

14. Are you a woman of prayer? (vv 17-18)

15. Do you go after the sinner? Do you share your faith? (vv 19-20)

TWENTY TESTS OF SELF-EXAMINATION FROM FIRST JOHN

1. Test of joy: 1:4.
2. Test of having partnership or fellowship with Christ and the Father: 1:3.
3. Test of confessing our sins: 1:9.
4. Test of broken pattern of sinning: 2:1; 3:4-6; 3:8 9; 5:18.
5. Test of obedience: 2:3-5; 3:22-24; 5:2, 3.
6. Test of walking as Christ walked: 2:6.
7. Test of loving the brethren: 2:9-11; 3:10-18; 3:23; 4:7-12; 4:20-5:2.
8. Test of overcoming the wicked one: 2:13, 14; 5:4, 18.
9. Test of not loving the world: 2:15-17; 4:5.
10. Test of persevering to the end: 2:19, 24.
11. Test of the indwelling Holy Spirit: 2:20, 27; 3:24; 4:13.
12. Test of belief: 2:23; 3:23; 4:2, 15; 5:1, 2, 5,10,13,20.
13. Test of abiding in Him: 2:27, 28; 4:16.
14. Test of holy living: 2:29; 3:3, 7.
15. Test of hatred from the world: 3:13.
16. Test of answered prayer: 3:22; 5:14, 15.
17. Test of overcoming false teachers: 4:4.
18. Test of no fear in judgment: 2:28; 4:17, 18.
19. Test of loving God: 4:19-5:2.
20. Test of keeping ourselves from idols: 5:21.